A Gift So Rare

A Gift So Rare

MORE INSPIRATIONAL VERSES

BY HELEN LOWRIE MARSHALL

WITH ILLUSTRATIONS

BY MURIEL WOOD

HALLMARK EDITIONS

A Gift So Rare

PRELUDE

The harmony of Heaven fills the air,
   As softly now the organ lifts its prayer.

THE PRIVILEGE OF LIVING

Thank God for the privilege of living,
The privilege of breathing the air,
The privilege of being alive in the midst
Of such beauty everywhere!
Thank the good Lord for His mercy
In giving me eyes to see,
A mind to learn, and a voice to speak
And a faith in Eternity.
Thank God for the privilege of living—
For sharing His earth and His sky—
That a gift so rare as the gift of life
Is given to such as I.

APRIL

There's a feeling of promise in the air,
A feeling of promise everywhere—
A promise of singing birds and bees,
A promise of fruit on barren trees.

A promise of gardens blooming gay,
A promise of summer come one day,
A promise of warm and sunny skies,
A promise that nothing ever dies.

A promise of beauty yet unseen,
A promise of brown earth clothed in green,
A promise of warmth and light and cheer,
A promise of hope this time of year.

THANKS GIVING

I tried—I tried so very hard to pray,
To thank God for this lovely, lovely day;
But, as I knelt, so many blessings grew,
It seemed as though my heart would burst in two
With thankfulness—so many blessings there
To crowd into just one small "Thank you" prayer;
But as my lips groped haltingly to find
The words to speak my humbly grateful mind,
I heard God's gentle whisper, kneeling there,
"Arise my child, thy heart has said thy prayer."

A HEAVEN EVERY DAY

What wondrous miracles abound
   In ordinary things.
And yet how casually we sing
   And hear a world that sings.
A rosebud bursts its prison pod
   And fragrance fills the air—
The tender grasses break the sod
   And green is everywhere.

A daisy lifts its dazzling smile
   To blue skies high above—
The maiden plucks the petals off
   And dreams of her true love.
A baby takes a faltering step—
   A brave soul smiles through pain.
The summer dies—the white snow flies—
   And spring is born again.

A universe of miracles,
   So very commonplace
We take them all for granted
   And accept with careless grace.
With wistful eyes we visualize
   A Heaven far away,
The while we stumble blindly through
   A heaven every day.

TAKE MY HAND

Are you troubled, burdened, blue?
   Take my hand.
I've been troubled, burdened, too,
   I understand.
Where you've fallen, once I fell—
Oh, I know these pitfalls well.
Let me help the clouds dispel—
   Take my hand.

Others helped when I was weak,
   Took my hand,
Helped me face toward the peak,
   Helped me stand.
What they did, now let me do—
Pass that kindness on to you.
Some day you'll help others, too.
   Take my hand.

MORE TIME TO LIVE

We ought to take more time to live—
More time to really see
The glory and the wonders of this earth;
The quiet, gentle beauty,
The sheer nobility
Revealed alone to those who prize its worth.
We ought to take more time to care—
To really, truly care,
Enough to fling our heart's door open wide;
To lend a helping hand and share
The burdens others bear,
And take the poor and comfortless inside.
We ought to take more time to feel—
To surely, deeply feel
The quiet depth and power of God's love;
The close-enfolding presence of His peace,
Profound and real,
The faith that lifts the soul to heights above.
We ought to take more time to live—
To wholly, truly live,
More time to feel and care, more time to see;
To fully realize the endless joys
That life can give,
To laugh—and love—and live abundantly!

THE WONDER OF IT ALL

There are so many small, incessant things—
The constant whir of tiny unseen wings,
The steady beat of hearts too small to hear—
That never reach the conscious eye or ear.

The crack of seedlings breaking through the pod,
The tender grasses pushing through the sod;
The bustle of the world down underground,
The air above so full of soundless sound.

The world within a world, where lives repeat
Their own small cycles, infinite, complete;
The unseen, steady flow of death and birth—
The business of an ever-changing earth.

The order and the wonder of it all—
A universe so great—a world so small!

LOVE-WIDE AND HEAVEN-HIGH

My world was little and cozy-tight,
Snug and smug in its dim half-light;
And, though it was too small inside
For me to stretch my arms out wide
Or let me stand up straight and tall,
This annoyed me not at all.
I crouched in my small world each day,
Content to doze the hours away—
Till a stray sunbeam, quite lost, I'm sure,
Found its way through a crack in my door.
A wandering thought it might have been,
But it shone with a brightness I'd never seen,
And it lighted my world's dimlit way
And it tempted me forth to a sunbright day.
I opened the door and stepped outside
Into a new world, high and wide!
With outstretched arms to embrace it all,
I felt my soul stand straight and tall!
And I knew that I could never go back
To that little world with its pitiful lack
Of all that made life glow and shine,
Now that this wider world was mine.
So I closed the door and I turned the key
On that little world and that little me,
And I raised my face to the open sky
In a world love-wide and Heaven-high!

SOMETIMES A STAR

May the rains of life that fall upon
    Your spirits now and then,
Leave behind them pools of light
    To make life bright again,
Clean and shining pools of light
    Reflecting Heaven's blue,
And possibly sometimes a star
To light the way for you.

THERE'LL BE ANOTHER SPRING

There'll be another spring, I know,
When flowers will replace the snow,
When birds will waken me at dawn
And pain and sorrow will be gone—
    There'll be another spring.

There'll be another day in June,
When, once more, life will be in tune,
When I will raise my eyes and see
A whole blue sky made just for me.
    There'll be another June.

And, till that June and springtime come,
I'll close my ears against the strum
Of wind and sleet upon the pane,
The cold, the loneliness—and then
    There'll be another spring.

PATIENCE

"Things have a way of working out,"
    My father used to say.
"Don't force the issue. Do your best
    And work and wait and pray."

How many times those words return
    When life's a tangled thread—
"Just do your best today, and leave
    To God the days ahead."

Somewhere a Master Planner works,
    Though how we may not know,
But in due time things will work out—
    The years have proved it so.

TRUE MEASURE

How long we live is not for us to say;
We may have years ahead—or but a day.
The length of life is not of our control,
But length is not the measure of the soul—
Not length, but width and depth define the span
By which the world takes measure of a man.
It matters not how long before we sleep,
But only how wide is our life—how deep.

ALMOST A MEMORY

What is it that the song awakes in me?
Almost a tear—almost a memory;
A fleeting, lonely something that evades,
A glimmering of memory that fades
And vanishes as I pursue—and yet,
Something it is my heart cannot forget.

What is this haunting thing within the strain
That stirs some deep, long buried, hidden pain
Within the heart of me—a yearning there?
My groping fingers clutch the empty air,
The ghost uncaptured, unrevealed—and yet,
Something it is my heart cannot forget.

And now the song has ended—quiet falls,
And I am left still wandering the halls
Of reverie, lost in my fruitless quest
Of half-remembered things locked in my breast.
What is it that the song awakes in me?
Almost a tear—almost a memory.

DARE TO BE DIFFERENT

Dare to be different; life is so full
Of people who follow the same push-and-pull,
Poor, plodding people who, other than name,
Try to pretend they're exactly the same.

God made men different; there never will be
A replica soul made of you or of me.
The charm—the glory of all creation
Rests on this very deviation.

Your charm—your own glory, too,
Lies in being uniquely you—
Lies in being true to your best,
That part of you different from all of the rest.

CAUSE AND EFFECT

Once, someone said something nice about me,
And, all undeserved though I knew it to be,
I treasured it there on my heart's deepest shelf,
Till one day I quite surprised even myself
By honestly making an effort to be
That nice thing that somebody said about me!

REASON FOR BEING

I would look deep within
This living book I call Myself.
I would dust off the cover,
Lift it down from Life's high shelf;
Would delve deep into chapters
That long ago were closed,
And bring to light the secrets
Never honestly exposed.
I would study it for lessons
That should be recorded there.
I would test it for its value—
Is it honest? Is it fair?
I would search to find the answer
Why this book is on Life's Shelf—
I would hope to find the reason
For this book I call Myself.

MY ALTAR

I have a little altar in my heart—
A corner set aside, a shrine apart;
And oh, a dozen times or more a day
I find me stealing quietly away
To kneel before my little altar there
And offer up a thought or two in prayer—
A little "Thank you, God" when things go right;
A prayer for light to guide me through the night;
A plea for strength to help me right the wrong;
Or sometimes, maybe, just a bit of song.
I have a little altar in my heart—
A corner set aside, a shrine apart,
A quiet place where I find sweet release
From daily care—and strength and joy and peace.

HOLY GROUND

On what divergent paths man seeks the heights,
How many different roadways has he trod
Upward and ever up, since time began,
His face turned to the sun and stars—and God.

And wise is he who sees the worth of all,
For beauty lies in all ways men have found.
And none is perfect, none without a flaw—
Yet every pathway there—is Holy Ground.

THE HUMANIST

"I'm not a praying man," he says,
    And quite believes it, too,
But you can always count on him
    When there is work to do;
He's right there with a helping hand
    Whenever there is need,
When there are children to be clothed
    Or hungry mouths to feed.

He's not a praying man, he says,
    And yet I've seen him share
With others, giving cheerfully,
    When he had none to spare;
I've heard him speak a kindly word
    When slander flew about,
And lend his quiet courage
    To the fellow down and out.

I've seen him watch a sunset,
    And listen to a song;
I've heard his friendly whistle
    When a stray dog came along—
Because of him, the world's
    A little better place today—
And yet he quite believes it
    When he says he doesn't pray!

MY DAY

This be my day—
Some honest work,
A bit of play—
To laugh and love,
And live and pray
With God beside me
All the way—
This be my day.

AND HE SAW NOT

He boasted unbelief,
And scorned the Deity—
    And all the while he sat beneath
    A flowering apple tree.

He said there was no proof
Of God—that no one knows—
    And all the while he idly smelled
    The fragrance of a rose.

He scoffed at pious folk
Who prattle of God's grace—
    And all the while he looked into
    A baby's upturned face.

A MINUTE TO SPEND

So you have only a minute to spend?
Well, here's what a minute will buy—
A word to let someone know that you care,
A smile to a passer by,
A bit of communion with God and His world,
A "thank you" that's maybe long due,
A deep look inward to change your sights
And broaden your point of view.
If you have all of a minute to spend,
How very lucky you are!
For a minute will buy a whole heart's prayer,
And pay your way clean to a star!

I KNOW

You say there is no proof that God exists;
'Tis but a supposition—no one knows.
Oh, but you're wrong, my friend, so very wrong.
There's proof enough. I know. I've seen a rose.

BACK FROM THE ROAD

Let me go back from the traveled road
Away from the crowds pushing by,
To a quiet hill where the woods are still,
Serene 'neath a clean, blue sky.

I would go back, far back from the road,
Away from the haunts of men,
I would find peace of mind
      where the hidden trails wind,
And strength to return again.

A FAITH THAT SMILES

Give us a faith in the worth of ourselves,
And faith in our fellow man;
Give us a faith that right will prevail
In the Infinite over-all plan;
Give us a faith in the future—
A farmer's faith in the sod,
A faith in Eternal justice
A faith in the love of God;
Give us a faith for the journey of life,
A strength for the winding miles,
A faith to sustain—but above all, Lord,
Give us a faith that smiles!

SELF-SEARCHING

A part of me I own, but only part;
There still are deep recesses in my heart,
And vast uncharted wastelands in my mind
I must explore, and search until I find
The rest of me; when I possess my soul,
Then—then will I be whole.

OF WHAT HE WILL

How haloed are the joys of Yesterday
Through misty mauve of memory defined;
How gently time erases, dims the way
That things unpleasant may be lost to mind;
How zealously the heart guards fleeting pleasure
And casts aside the bitterness and pain;
Looks back to Yesterday to find its measure
For building up its hope and faith again.
How tenderly the Father has provided
The soul of man with liberty to choose—
To find the good in all the many-sided,
And salvage that of life he can best use.

The Past stands by, a bank where man may borrow
Of what he will to shape his own Tomorrow.

ESPECIALLY FOR YOU

"I made it 'specially for you,"
  He said, and handed me
The dubious daub of color
  He had made for me to see.

A horse? A cat? A fish? A shoe?
  Who quibbles with such art?
No matter what it was I knew
  It came straight from his heart.

I told him it was beautiful—
  I loved his big surprise!
And a million dollars couldn't buy
  That pleased look in his eyes.

"Especially for you"—three words
  Such potent magic hold,
They turn the smallest gift on earth
  To one of purest gold.

A DREAM IS FOREVER

A dream is forever—spurn it if you will—
Somewhere in your heart there's a part of it still;
Somewhere there's an echo—a smile or a sigh,
Recalling that long-ago dream that passed by.

A dream is forever—it can't be erased;
And richer the life that a dream has embraced,
Warmer the heart that has felt the bright beam
Of life-giving hope shining forth in a dream.

WHEN WINTER COMES

When winter comes, I shall remember
    This glorious day in May.
In the chill of life's coldest December,
    I shall be warmed that way.

I shall be warmed by the sunshine
    Of a world attuned to Spring;
I shall see apple trees in bloom,
    I shall hear robins sing.

No matter how the winds buffet,
    No matter how deep the snow,
Life's beauty outweighs its bitter—
    Remembering—I shall know.

WINDOWS OF THE MIND

The dream precedes the deed—
    A boy must dream;
As youth must first see greatness
    In his scheme.
And, even though the dreaming
    Goes too far—
No one is hurt by reaching
    Toward a star.

And if the deed fall short?
    A little fall
Is better than no dream,
    No deed, at all.
The dream precedes the deed,
    And youth will find
That dreams are really windows
    Of the mind.

WINDOW SHOPPING

I drive the quiet, lonely street,
Past homes with lights agleam,
And trials of the day seem to melt away
As I windowshop for a dream.

I glimpse the warmth and happiness
Bathed in their sea of light,
Pictures of home—the heart's desire,
Framed in the lonely night.

And my faith in the rightness of things returns,
In the fitness of God's great scheme,
And my heart remembers its song of hope
As I windowshop for a dream.

AROUND THE BEND

We never know what waits around the bend;
The Master Planner must have planned it so,
That we may fully savor each day's blend
Of happiness and sadness as we go.

For even joy's full flavor would be lost
Were it not given us in morsel size;
And sorrow would exact too great a cost,
Were not tomorrow's pain screened from our eyes.

There is a comfort comes with each day's end,
A hope that clings to things beyond our sight.
We never know what waits around the bend—
It is enough that dawn shall follow night.

THESE ARE THE DAYS

These are the days—these autumn days,
    When memories haunt us most;
When our Yesterday's Self goes wandering
    Like a restless little ghost
Down long-forgotten pathways
    Of things that used to be,
Vainly trying to fasten leaves
    Back on a bare-blown tree.

These are the days—these leaf-strewn days,
    When poignant hours we've known
Toll the heart's most solemn bell
    With deep and mournful tone;
When restless yearnings bare the soul
    As fall winds bare the trees,
Till, lonely and alone, it stands,
    A prey to winter's breeze.

These are the days—these frost-filled days,
    For which the spring was born,
For which the summer gave her bloom—
    The evening of the morn.
These are the days—these sere, brown days,
    When man is given to see
The cycle of the universe
    And his own destiny.

But oh, these, too, are golden days,
　　With beauty unsurpassed—
Days when our life brings forth its yield
　　Of riches from the past;
Days when the golden wealth of joys
　　And tears that we have sown
Has reached its ripe fruition—
　　To strength and beauty grown.

These are the days—the harvest days,
　　When life is rich and whole—
The spirit's golden bounty days.
　　Fulfillment of the soul.

TRULY BLEST

Have you felt that special stillness,
That solemn, reverent hush
That settles on the earth
   At close of day;
As though the world had come to rest
In all its frenzied rush
And paused for one short moment
   Just to pray?

Have you sensed the awesome beauty,
The deep, pervading peace
That seems to fill the heart
   To overflow;
When all its pent-up love pours forth
In blessed, sweet release
Within that holy light
   Of evenglow?

If you've known this benediction,
Felt its calming in your soul,
Then you've come closer than
   You may have guessed
To the very gates of Heaven
Where you've been renewed, made whole,
And you have walked among those
   Truly blest.

TOMORROW

Tomorrow does not stand apart,
    A shining, all new day;
Tomorrow is a thing slow-built
    Of hours passed away.

It's made of dreams your heart has stored,
    And dreams discarded, too;
It's made of all the joys and tears
    The years have brought to you.

It's made of lessons you have learned,
    The friends you've known—the foes;
As each of our Todays is bent,
    So our Tomorrow grows.

It's made of sweat and toil and pain
    And song and love and laughter;
Each minute of Today helps build
    The day that follows after.

Tomorrow does not spring full-built
    With some new dawn's bright rays—
Tomorrow is a slow-built thing
    Made up of Yesterdays.

INDEX

A GIFT SO RARE

Set at The Castle Press in Linotype Aldus, a roman with
old-face characteristics, designed by Hermann Zapf.
Aldus was named for the 16th century Venetian
printer Aldus Manutius.
Printed on Hallmark Eggshell Book paper.
Designed by Harriett Hanson.